Sunset and Blizzard

Sunset and Blizzard

Experiencing Lent

DANIEL RUY PEREIRA

RESOURCE *Publications* • Eugene, Oregon

SUNSET AND BLIZZARD
Experiencing Lent

Resource Publications
An Imprint of Wipf and Stock Publishers
199 W. 8th Ave., Suite 3
Eugene, OR 97401

www.wipfandstock.com

PAPERBACK ISBN: 978-1-5326-6444-1
HARDCOVER ISBN: 978-1-5326-6445-8
EBOOK ISBN: 978-1-5326-6446-5

Manufactured in the U.S.A. 11/27/18

All other quotations are from the Book of Common Prayer, from "The Daily Prayer App" by Church House Publishing and AIMER.

Contents

Preface

Peace be with you.

I had experienced Lent twice. In 2018 I stopped feeling uncomfortable about it and Lent had become something I was looking forward to. The sole reason is: my life had been (and still is) hectic. I teach, write, study, pay bills, look after my daughter, spend time with my wife and a lot more.

Do I have time for God?

I don't mean just praying in the morning, before going to bed, or before meals. I mean spending actual time. Whenever I stop what I am doing, do I seek solace, pleasure and joy in Him?

At least for 40 days, I intended to.

I struggled a bit with the idea of writing one poem a day, because Lent is about humility, whereas in the end, writing poems is about doing my best and being proud of my work. However, Lent is also a time of fasting in which I hope to help people to come closer to God, as I am trying to do myself. So, I wanted my writing to help someone think about how wonderful a Person God is.

When the season started, I prayed the following prayer – which I continued to pray every single day until the end of the fast.

> Blessed are you, God of compassion and mercy,
> to you be praise and glory for ever.
> In the darkness of our sin,
> your light breaks forth like the dawn
> and your healing springs up for deliverance.
> As we rejoice in the gift of your saving help,
> sustain us with your bountiful Spirit
> and open our lips to sing your praise.
> Blessed be God, Father, Son and Holy Spirit.

Blessed be God for ever.

Why does this prayer appears every day, a mixture of humility, sadness and darkness but then rejoicing, praise and blessing? I set out to answer that question for myself. Now, fast-forward 48 days and you'll see me praying this:

Lord, you let your servant go in peace:
your word has been fulfilled.
My own eyes have seen the salvation
which you have prepared
in the sight of every people;
a light to reveal you to the nations
and the glory of your people Israel. (Luke 2:29–32)

What happened in between? Quite an experience. I wrote 44 poems in 48 days, starting on Ash Wednesday every single day until Easter Sunday. When I started this project, my aim was to live my Lent and, at the end of each day, reflect on the entire day, pray, conduct my Bible reading or meditate on events that happened somewhere in the world.

This is how it went.

At the start, I intended to pray three times daily. I failed. I also wanted to eat healthily and avoid fast foods. In that, I also failed. I did not read comic books, as I had promised – but I read strip comics and even produced some for my pupils at school. I did not play videogames – except a brief 5 minutes of a racing game at my local library. I failed on that one too.

I think I pretty much failed on everything that I set out to do; I had given up on everything, except for writing my poems, one poem every day. The type of reflection that came from it was, sometimes confronting, sometimes humbling.

I tried to control my hunger for fame and I did not promote the original blog that first displayed the poems, except by linking it to some of my social media accounts. I prayed that God would bring people in the open environment of the Internet to follow my quest with me. The reason I did that was to cultivate humility in me and to dedicate those poems to God.

But poetry is an exercise on how to improve yourself every day, and often I was carried away by presenting an idea in a new style or the rhyme scheme, or the freeform or whatnot. At the end I decided to stick with the Brazilian form called *cordel*, for the last sections, because I think it could fit neatly into the idea I had been brewing to tell those stories. I wanted to do well. Was I proud? I don't know. If so, may God forgive me.

So, all said and done, was it a positive experience?

Most definitely. My soul was closer to God. I wanted to please Him. I wanted to try harder and harder, until I could be satisfied with the praise I was offering up. I just wish that this could be the norm, not the exception.

One day, though, I trust it will be.

Lent is about struggling with your soul, but keeping your eyes on Jesus, and constantly recalling our ultimate hope. It doesn't have to be only before Easter, though – any time can be transformed into Lent.

May He use these poems to start a conversation with you too.

My time of quiet reflection is over. I want to share my experience now.

May the risen Lord Jesus bless us.
May he watch over us and renew us
as he renews the whole of creation.
May our hearts and lives echo his love.
Amen.

Daniel Ruy Pereira
Lent, 2018

Acknowledgements

THIS BOOK WOULD NOT have been possible without some invaluable people, their experience, care and feedback.

Firstly, thank you Angelica and Sophia, my girls, for understanding my absence when writing and supporting me when I need silence to calm my mind. I love you both.

Second, thank you Amanda Martin, Bob Springett, Natasha Rawling and Cláudio Bispo for the copyediting and critique. It would be an entirely different book without you. Actually, it wouldn't be a book hadn't you stepped in to help me with grammar, structure, dialect etc. God bless you.

I also thank the lovely people from Wipf and Stock, who believed in this project and turned it into a beautiful product.

I am indebted to a number of authors who publish the amazing cordel style in Brazil. I got to know it when I was a teenager, however I am privileged to have spent my honeymoon in Pernambuco, where I bought several pamphlets, which I still own, and kept stirring ideas in my brain ever since. The late João Cabral de Melo Neto became a huge influence to my poems, specially the last ones in this volume – but the small 32 stanza poems by not widely known authors I used to buy in Sao Paulo town centre when I was younger led me here. Obrigado cordelistas! We are all Severinos, equals in everything in our lives and lots.

Is this the kind of fast I have chosen,
only a day for people to humble themselves?
Is it only for bowing one's head like a reed
and for lying in sackcloth and ashes?
Is that what you call a fast,
a day acceptable to the Lord?
(Isaiah 58:5)

Ash Valentine

Let him kiss me with the kisses of his mouth—
for your love is more delightful than wine.
(Song of Songs 1:2)

Today is Valentine.
No flowers nor wine
No night out with her
No ring polisher

Asleep as an angel
I see my dear wife–
I go mind my life
moving but frozen.

'I didn't wake her,'
I think while I stir
my tea, brain and heart
wishing to restart

Today is Ash Wednesday
And I am so sad
No rest. A Nomad
Making my own way

I lose my balance
When I hear silence
Echoing my iced core–
Longa rest that roars

I realise now:
It's a Holy Day
Sadness has the weight
Of thorns on his brow

My gift is broken
    A cheap bad token
That I call 'my soul'–
    That you call 'my goal'

Today is Valentine
    Date with the Divine
A night out with God
    His love, staff and rod

Questions for Lent

> At once the Spirit sent him out into the wilderness, and he was in the wilderness forty days, being tempted by Satan. He was with the wild animals, and angels attended him.
>
> (Mark 1:12–13)

Am I that humble?
  Do I feel I stumble?
    Does my heart crumble?
      Am I a true Christian?

Do I offer my prayers?
  My time? Do I share?
    Do I think and compare?
      Do I stop and listen?

Do I sow? Do I weep?
  Am I awake or asleep?
    Is my faith that deep?
      Or is it just tradition?

How then will I serve?
  Do I have the nerve?
    Is Lent just "to observe"?
      Will I take on the mission?

One year

Teach us to number our days,
that we may gain a heart of wisdom.
(Psalm 90:12)

1
a young family
sat on the church entrance's steps.
Ice cream and laughter.

2
children toss leaves up,
watching them fly and fall again.
Wheezing grandpa laughs.

3
frozen ground and hail.
packed hospital waiting room–
the priest sits alone

4
daisies popping up
in the church's old graveyard.
the brand new headstone

Seal of Approval

Those who flatter their neighbours
are spreading nets for their feet.
(Proverbs 29:5)

The other day I was feeling not okay.
At home, alone,
I put the kettle on for two.
One tea for me,
the other one for my self.

I told my self I was afraid of collapsing.
    "Never fear," said my self.
"But I don't think I am actually that good."
    "Never doubt."
"I am not even sure of what I'm doing."
    "Never critique!"
"I should just give up, I think."
    "Don't be too demanding."
"I'll have to surrender to God."
    "Don't—either you follow my lead and emerge prosperous
    or you turn into a humble mess.
    Why doesn't God cut you some slack?"
Well, I don't know
Should I believe my self?

Disobedience

Why do you call me, 'Lord, Lord,' and do not do what I say?
(Luke 6:46)

She was so sad
    I wanted to hug her
But etiquette forbad

I wanted to comfort her
    But professionally, it would look bad

I wanted to understand her
    But reasons were obscure and mad

I wanted to cry for her . . .
    But I was so glad

I wanted to remember her
    But my mind was busy

I wanted to care for her
    But still, I think of myself

Old friend

. . . how can one keep warm alone? (Ecclesiastes 4:11)

There was a friend
        buried in the dirt
(a very old dirt):
        fossil, trapped.
It was unhurt.
        Awed scientists
looked at the friend:
        quite the novel trend.
it was extinct!

The paper issued
        described "the friend."
Explained traits,
        looked at genes.
It was the talk of the day
        It was the novelty

Collectors fought
        In auctions, in thought.
Money? Not an issue
        One spent fortunes
Buying the dead friend

Hanging on a wall
        We glance at it now
no longer new.

        Back to daily life

The Flip Side

Do not neglect your gift . . .
(1 Timothy 4:14)

I want to spend time with my daughter.
    I think of her all day long
Her blonde hair, her lovely laughter
    Read her a book? Sing her a song?
I'll teach her to be different from myself
    and love other people as she'll love herself.

The hectic day is finally over.
    As a cheetah in a hurry
I speed up as I get closer
    My mind sees her; all else is blurry
Cannot wait to see that wonderful warm smile!
    Every mile I cycle is another trial

Alas! I'm home! Keys turn with my mind
    from daily tasks to my little girl:
Spotted! I approach from behind,
    'Hello!', while stroking her curls.
My love overflows like a bath forgotten

My baby shoots me with an indifference shotgun
I am sold-out for those cheap cartoons
    Inhuman sounds, animal faces
She'd rather have idle afternoons
    Than my encompassing embrace
It really hurts to know how much I love her
    But she'd rather have TV to her loving father

Two flowers

. . . if I have a faith that can move mountains,
but do not have love, I am nothing.
(1 Corinthians 13:2)

The first flower cost a lot of money.
    Purple, posh, paid for with a pile of cash,
Chosen in only an hour, wrapped in gunny.
    "What need for panache if love's been smashed?"
Then the second flower costs only some change.
    Small, not tall, bought with a pinch of salt
After sour regret, wrapping love–not rage
    "I know I fell short. Will you forgive my fault?"

One week later, the posh flower was dead.
    Wilted, forgotten in a dark corner
with no nutrition, its roots couldn't spread

Two weeks later, the humble flower is blooming
    Colourful, on a ledge a lot warmer
with healthy roots over an eternal warm spring

CHANGE

> The wind blows wherever it pleases. You hear its sound, but you cannot tell where it comes from or where it is going. So it is with everyone born of the Spirit.
>
> (John 3:8)

She climbs up the stairs
and every step is in sync
with a drop, which tears
her soul apart–makes it shrink.
One half wants to stay
The other wants to go.
Her feet do not obey
and have a life of their own.
She flies up as Icarus.
Yet, her heart loves the ground
and her feet, as Daedalus,
just wants to make it count.
After so many summers
On the same piece of planet,
She knows: that newcomer
has crushed her old habits.
She's unknown to herself.
The answer she seeks
Is not on a bookshelf.
Wisdom is with the meek:
They shall inherit the earth.
She shall find herself again
in the moment of her rebirth–
Relief comes after the pain

About Afterlife

"But God said to him, 'You fool! This very night your life will be demanded from you. Then who will get what you have prepared for yourself?'

(Luke 12:20)

Every year,
fifty-five million
plus.

People die.

Eyes pointed up to the sky
they fear they might just survive
in hope, or gloom, asking "why?"
So, as time goes by,
many of them seem to thrive,
accumulating treasure;
some spend no effort, some strive;
some with tears, some with pleasure,
thinking they can duck the Dive
all take: bee, queen, or hive.

I wish the sarcophagus
could indeed be my sweet boat beyond.

Why! Why does death bother us so?

I know the answer quite well:
See, I doubt reincarnation,
the idea just doesn't sell.
The soul's evolution
lies after the farewell?
So why does man not excel?

Afterlife is populated
with virgins, angels, demons.

So will you be satisfied
in one of those Edens?
You might well be disappointed

Of all the heavens presented
You have to choose one or none,
but will you hit the jackpot?
When all things are said and done
will you be okay with what you got?
Will it be awful or fun?

The paradise begun
the day you were born to die
and when you died to be reborn.
Realise you cannot apply
to heaven, for nails and thorns
are our payment—you and I.
If only God could supply
someone to rightly lead us
on a path of certainty . . .
Some kind of Zeus or Phoebus.

I'd give my life for eternity!

The Sunset and the Blizzard

In repentance and rest is your salvation,
in quietness and trust is your strength . . .
(Isaiah 30:15)

After a rough, laborious shift,
I notice the merciful sunset–
The universe wrapped as a gift
behind the dark trees, beyond empty threats.

Ominous snowflakes slowly fall,
Shading the orange that goes away;
Grinning, dark curtains of ice crawl
with my thoughts, words and deeds of today
but the sunlight is not done with me yet–
The full-blown blizzard of consciousness
offers a challenge still to be met.
The sunset of mercy, nevertheless,
Keeps shining, not a bit upset,
Veering blizzards to come and bless

The nightmare

A dream comes when there are many cares . . .
(Ecclesiastes 5:3)

Some nightmares are actual dreams.
The one I dreamt about
Had me standing ashore with
a rocky core and a cold bloodstream.
I see everything without
my eyes or lens-and there's more!
The sand grains have my face!
They are wicked. Proud liars.
Pointing their fingers at me,
Laughing hard at my disgrace
With their sharp mockery daggers.
I can't fight the bully back

The grains of sand aggregate
In a matter of seconds!
They become a huge monster!
To him I am but a maggot–
It's not like in the legends:
I am my own mad butcher.

To the hills I go, stumbling,
the mad giant in pursuit.
I climb up and avoid the rocks;
My muscles and bones blazing,
My chest-pump irresolute
'Brave, aren't you?', the monster mocks

Exhausted, I glimpse at the peak
And on it, I see a vine
Surrounded by ripe wheat fields.
The hilltop is so unique
I scream: 'I've found Nature's shrine!'

Terror the monster wields:
He proclaims my sins, my violence.

I shiver and quit my quest
Falling, heavy as my heart.

The monster brags in silence
turning and facing the west
The big Monster-me departs

I prepare for damnation
when a flight of seven doves
Rescue me from my falling.
The seven turned to one
and told me I'm one it loves –
A love so deep that it stings

To the vine I am taken
Its sweet fruit I drink with bread
And have a wonderful time.
A delicious, holy fun
The Monster-me I see dead—
Joy weeping for atoned crimes!

Some nightmares are actual dreams
Bittersweet experiences
That make waking up a mess
When life is a house of screams
My joyful deliverance
Comes from that nightmare—my bless

They, Me and Him

I have listened attentively,
but they do not say what is right.
None of them repent of their wickedness,
saying, "What have I done?"
Each pursues their own course
like a horse charging into battle.
(Jeremiah 8:6)

I read in Jeremiah about these people
whose worship is bad, false, unstable, feeble:
greed, pride, backsliding, fondness of deceit,
a muddy moral soil, in which they dip their feet;
Truly proficient in the language of perjury,
they refuse any journey towards purity
Their impious deeds
like the stampede of a mad herd of cattle,
or horses plunging headlong into battle.

'Now the best course of action,' said Jeremiah,
would not be waiting for a D.I.Y. Messiah
but to concede God's brutal judgment,
filled with terror and cholera's scent.'
It's grim, yet the advice
could not be more precise,
since I've done twice as bad with a will of ice.

I want to stop there, seeing God as a tyrant,
a roaring, mighty lion, both his paws violent!

Instead,
I see a meek lamb,
both hands pierced.
He walked towards me.
My forehead he kissed,
telling me to lay down

my concerns,
my burden,
my life
because he has solved the problem,
ended the strife;

I, lost sheep, hurt in despair, hurt by choice.
He, my relentless shepherd,
hurt in hope, my lost voice.
Jeremiah was right: peace is a delusion
without God's scandalous grace –
Christ's Passion:
Where the Almighty God's brutal judgment
(filled with terror and cholera's scent) –
would hit they, you and I as hard as a cyclone
but there's Jesus,
enduring it
alone

Metamorphosis

Go to the ant, you sluggard;
consider its ways and be wise!
(Proverbs 6:6)

alas!
look at them:
ants, out and about
wasps—mighty stings
caterpillars, gluttons!
moths, posing as butterflies
black widows and slaughterers
slugs that move only when needed
cockroaches, robbing food from others

just look at them.
now, look at him.

the olive tree ants ate
stung on hands and feet
eaten alive,
bit by bit, over time
but they did not
rob him of food–
he fed them
he rushed
towards the web
and drank their poison
they can live
for he died
and they can
change
through
Him

Love is Friction

. . . love covers over a multitude of sins . . .
(1 Peter 4:8)

Imagine friction didn't exist
We could move freely, with no exception,
    in the same wrong direction.
Our nature would not be able to resist.
But as an example of friction,
Love breaks down chest crashes,
    it's a buffer for smashes
    soaking the harm of collisions

Love sticks our feet to the ground
Allowing, also, handshakes;
It transfers heat to cold hugs
It enables the healing of a wound
It makes tectonic hearts quake
It overpowers smooth shrugs.

The gift

All those the Father gives me will come to me,
and whoever comes to me I will never drive away.
(John 6:37)

On a Good Friday, day like no other,
    A son's given a gift by his father.
Puzzled, I look closer—I am the parcel!
    Moreover, I never cease to marvel,
The wrapping paper is actually my own skin,
    abounding with stains from my nature, my sin!

As the son rips and cuts through this first layer
    He looks at me, listening to my painful prayer.
I ask for grace;
    He answers by ripping my muscles–
I scream loud in anguish as my flesh struggles;
    His compassion reaches me, collecting my tears,
Whilst his hard nails dig
    into my organs as spears
My deafening shrieks cause him to weep bitterly
    but my eyes see him as a monster,
        cruel,
        chilly.

Then he glimpses my heart–
    Oh, I can't take it anymore!
I feel like a crushed slug lying on the floor

He stares at me
        waiting for a decision
Could this tortured soul bear that incision?
    Whatever I decide it'll be the end of this . . .
His pierced hands talk to me and I say:
    "Please."

(I have consciously decided my own death)

His scalpel's cut takes away my last breath
        Delight at the sight of his longed-for present:.
The first Prince to cherish a simple peasant

Gentleness

Be wise in the way you act toward outsiders;
make the most of every opportunity.
(Colossians 4:5)

A handsome baby was delivered
Because the doctor volunteered

The doctor, that day, was working
Because of the brief money-giving

That petty money was then given
Because some people still listen

Some people, therefore, showed care
Because a preacher was aware

The preacher was godly and true
For his mum had her prayers in her shoes

The mum's prayers were so moist and rife
Because one day, Christ Jesus gave his life

So every moment, centuries stand compressed
into a closed hand that is put to a test

Shame and Pride

Though you have made me see troubles,
many and bitter,
you will restore my life again;
from the depths of the earth
you will again bring me up.
(Psalm 71:20)

I've done something I am not proud of.
I've done something I am not. Proud.
I've done something I am not.
I've done something I am.
I've done something, I.
I've done something.
I've done it.
I have.
I.

You.
You have.
You have done it.
You have done something, you.
You have done something you are.
You have done something you are, humble.
You have done something: you have humbled me.

I've done something I am not happy with.
I've done something. I am not happy.
I've done something I am not.
I've done something I am.
I've done something, I.
I've done something.
I am done.
I am.
I.

You.
You are.
You have done it.
You have done something, you.
You have done something you are.
You have done something. You are mercy.
You have done something: you have forgiven me.

The calming of the storm

He stilled the storm to a whisper . . . (Psalm 107:29)

Clouds and thick darkness surround you, o God;
    You rule with righteousness and justice, Lord.
Why sometimes do I think you are a fraud?
    Instead of mercy, you unsheathe your sword.
Yesterday I prayed, but I felt ignored
    by your stupendous powerful kindness
(Am I such a bad tenant, oh Landlord,
    So afraid of serving you, Your Highness?)

Sometimes I think you see an arthropod
    Crawling a religion it can't afford!
I wonder if this thought is actually odd . . .
    Am I despicable, for the record?
Why do I feel like a minefield explored
    by my mindless brain and my blind retinas?
I begin to see hell as a fine reward,
    prone to believing my thoughts for once

My face feels like a derelict facade now
    This heart of mine as water that's been poured
Tears tearing my structure as a bold squad
Closed eyes see my soul healing in a ward
    My sinful words as a zombified horde
But the crucifix appears to me as the kindest
    symbol—the Fountain of Life so dead, so gored
The Breather of Life reduced to fine dust

Finally! Now I understand why those clouds nod:
    Darkness and sunbeams are in one accord
As I marvel at them at the esplanade—
    Please, pardon my sin, o just and merciful Lord.

Confession

Have mercy on me, O God,
according to your unfailing love;
according to your great compassion
blot out my transgressions.
Wash away all my iniquity
and cleanse me from my sin.
(Psalm 51:1–2)

Our holy God, our father, most merciful,
This day is closing, not a perfect end . . .
Here I approach your throne and pretend
I am not a bad person, not sinful.
My hands Lord Jesus I present: they are full
of blood, shame and deeds I cannot defend;
My mouth is full of lies and words that offend;
My brain a star of doubts—I feel hell's mighty pull

I sin in success, I sin in failure
Yet brave I come, to touch Emanuel's robe,
(my disgusting hands on a Person so pure)
but every day I ask you, Lord, to probe
my heart, which is so young and immature,
You know my soul; you walked upon this globe

To the Table

And he took bread, gave thanks and broke it, and gave it to them, saying, "This is my body given for you; do this in remembrance of me."

(Luke 22:19)

We do not presume to come to this your Table,
O merciful Lord, trusting in our own righteousness,
but in your manifold and great mercies . . .

"Lord, my spirit is crippled.
Every time I come to this diocese
My wheelchair is pushed by my worries."

. . . We are not worthy so much as
to gather up the crumbs
under your Table . . .

"Lord, my present is who I was—
My good intention succumbs
before my religion: only a fable."

. . . But you are the same Lord,
whose nature is always
to have mercy . . .

"Lord, how many times have I ignored
your law? How much the burden weighs!
I know how deep within me your eyes can see!"

. . . Grant us therefore, gracious Lord,
so to eat the flesh of your dear Son Jesus Christ,
and to drink his blood . . .

"Lord, are you really on board?
Why can't I see you through the mist?

Will there be peace after this flood?"

. . . That our sinful bodies may be made clean
by his body, and our souls washed
through his most precious blood . . .

"Lord, I have asked 'what does this mean?'
I have felt like an insect: squashed.
I have sunk down into a sinful mud."

. . . And that we may evermore
dwell in him,
and he in us. Amen.

"Lord, I recall my life before,
how my light used to be so dim.
But I thank you, I have been born again."

Morningstar

The heavens declare the glory of God;
the skies proclaim the work of his hands.
(Psalm 19:1)

Your colourless eyes gaze at mine:
    Black pupil surrounded by your iris,
Blind—luminous as Antares
    Such a gaze, so firm, so divine!
Penetrates like radiation,
    Altering my whole composition

From those eyes, a tear emerges,
    Dividing light into a rainbow
Like a balm river, it starts its flow;
    At the confluence with Weep, it surges–
I feel as Naaman hit by that tsunami.
    Then I am just myself—a soaked origami

When I recover my lost vision,
    Morningstar, I look full in your face
Looking back at this speck in Space.
    Outshining my old geocentric religion.
You pull me over towards you
    And I am accelerating too.

Timelessness

God said to Moses, "I am who I am. This is what you are to say to the Israelites: 'I am has sent me to you.'"

(Exodus 3:14)

You are my yesterday,
back when I began,
When
"I will be a better and more sensible man"–
"You have become my future," I would proclaim,
when I was worse than expected.
When I was still . . . just the same.

But you shall always be
my constant, my present tense
whether I move or stop
whether I am mild or intense
You are everything
I have not been working for.

My Conqueror, in this
soul-shattering war,
O, the achronism of your
love and grace!
So sublime
So sublime

Still
why do I claim
not to have much time?

Discipline

> I do not run like someone running aimlessly; I do not fight like a boxer beating the air. No, I strike a blow to my body and make it my slave so that after I have preached to others, I myself will not be disqualified for the prize.
>
> (1 Corinthians 9:26–27)

I was tired of being bullied by life.
So I enrolled my soul to train karate,
    to defend myself and, bravely, fight back.
Life is a master, though, in her own style
While I,
    on the other hand, am raw and spotty
My belt's merely white, Life's entirely black
She is a ruffian–strong and hostile,
    needs no weapon or muscular body.

So I needed a Master with a knack

I found one, hidden, in an alley
    Solitaire type, passing by me and everyone else
However, he was above proficiency:
    he demoed kicks and punches and, by the finale,
I was hooked and asked "what next?"
He said:
    "To overcome your deficiency I'm gonna take you to this valley full of shadow and death for your senses 'til you stop trusting your sufficiency." "If you wish to be my singular disciple do everything I say and follow my steps. Neither doubts nor flinching. Will you take it?"

I answered:

"Who else, from all people, could develop my spirit against this complex threat? I need to fight. Yes, I submit."

Then I saw myself in the mirror. How feeble!
That cruel Life had broken me down into flecks!

My master has been moulding me like a bonsai
Planting, pruning, wiring, and watering
Pushing my survival skills to the limits
He could only have set his bar so very high
Some days it felt like going through slaughtering
He never failed to notice my grimace.
So patient! Even when I wouldn't comply
And on the next day go out with me, sauntering
How many plasters, how many tourniquets!

Nowadays we're focusing on my posture:
Knees should be always flexed and hands folded
My only weapon is my Master's huge wisdom
Lifelong learning I must ensure.

What happened to Life?
Master scolded her.
Never again was I a victim.
I feel like an old bonsai tree—mature.
After my Master's image, he had me so moulded
I befriended life.
Our quibble's done.

Thanksgiving

Because of the Lord's great love we are not consumed,
for his compassions never fail.
They are new every morning;
great is your faithfulness.
(Lamentations 3:22–23)

My Father, thank you.
For the darkest night
In which my ideals
were all torn apart
by those sharpened thorns
in every single rose;
Thank you for the scars
and bitter memories.
Thank you, my Father,
for humility,
for friends and enemies
Thank you for my bad
health condition,
and for the treatment
That works so slowly.

I'm a combination
of scars and traumas:
pastors that preached
The best sermons
I've ever heard.

Thank you, my Father.
My Father. Thank you.

SAINT FRANCIS

> Remember your leaders, who spoke the word of God to you. Consider the outcome of their way of life and imitate their faith.
>
> (Hebrews 13:7)

Lord, bless the pastors who took care of me—
    dedicated lives to God, One-in-Three.
Make them the ploughs of love to plant new trees
    in soils such that even the seed disagrees;
Make them the sanitation against all the sludge
    that deposits in the heart, in the form of grudge;
In groups immune to unity, to sanity,
    please, let them be vaccines of affinity;
Appoint them as heralds for Lady Wisdom
    in times of uncertain extremism;
Dear Lord, turn my pastors
    into as shoots of hope
    to those whose despair is too much to cope;
Ignite them as light bulbs of new ideas
    in the cosy, but cold, stone rooms of tradition;
Brew them as ground coffee beans,
    from laughter soil,
    to your dear friends, whom life and sadness spoil.
After all, Lord, they only serve to console,
    for their fate is to be emptied so that they are made whole;
They suffer to be wells of understanding
    for judges and thecritic buckets they bring;
Help them to love; help them deal with despise;
When movements rise,
when they need to be wise;
To forgive when often abandoned;
Their Call is feet-washing, not be enthroned.
For their profession goes against all trends:
They love and give their lives to unknown friends

Collect

Grace and peace to you from God our Father and the Lord Jesus Christ.
(Ephesians 1:2)

Almighty and everlasting God,
There is nothing you cannot do
    And no right time for you to do it
You manage space-time as you see fit

To say you hate us is not untrue
    if we sin and never submit.
But when we humans are contrite,
    When our knees walk the extra mile
Your grin expands as the universe–
    Reason why stars produce more light.
We respond by showing even more guile
    Prouder, more selfish, bad—or worse!
Righteous Lord God, source of all mercy,
    I can't fathom why you forgive.
Why did you crush Jesus for our sake?
    Oh, praise this blessed controversy!
Through this paradox of love I live
    whether asleep, dreaming, awake.
Glory to the Father, to the Son
    And to the Most Holy Spirit,
As it was in the beginning, now
    and forever, God Three-in-one,
whose unbound love knows no limits,
    You love me but I don't know how

"Go," said Jesus, "your faith has healed you.""

(Mark 10:52)

Hurt

> For I know the plans I have for you," declares the LORD, "plans to prosper you and not to harm you, plans to give you hope and a future."
> (Jeremiah 29:11)

Often I feel sold away
        to be an alien, to be a slave.
Forgotten in a dungeon,
        a hated orc in a cave,
unfit for love or reason.
        Will this sinful moss be my grave?
Temptations coming in waves
        and I'm sailing a mere raft!
People are fair and futile
        Here they believe in witchcraft
(their religion so docile).
        I preached God. They laughed.
Why has my preaching been scoffed?
        Why am I even here, for starters,
When I just wanted my people?
        I shall tell you why: my own brothers
hated my dreams, loved evil;
        Were rascals to each other
You see, we're all minuscule critters:
Bees building a yellow hive,
        under one and only mighty Queen
to the world. Her honey we should drive.
        Instead, we sting with an obscene
judgement. How then can we thrive?

Well, if my spirit's still alive
        it's due to God using foul acts
to fulfil his plan–his bliss–
        For there are so many facts
that explain what a man is,
        And the unsung lives he impacts

Lonely

> "Turn to me and be gracious to me,
> for I am lonely and afflicted."
> (Psalm 25:16)

The ceiling in my room has some cracks
  through which I can see the growth of mould.
Specks of dust enjoy their chaos:
  glad, whether it's hot or cold
Not bothered with my pathos,
  oblivious to me getting old.
The way my calamities unfold
  add up to loneliness–
A swamp of noisy dragonflies
  and soft mire.
Nonetheless, it isn't calm.
  I agonize
having no one to confess my sins.
  Do I love God? Oh, yes.
His pardon I've received.
  Lacking is my brother of flesh,
my companion, who relieved
  my journey, making it afresh.
But him too life has seized—
  it didn't matter if I screamed
Then he was taken elsewhere
  and I was left with the bullies.
I have lifted up my prayer,
  I've appealed to the juries
of heaven about my despair,
  feeling like a hunted hare.
I'm alone! I'm so alone!

Oh, my dear brother, where are you?
  You are my muscle; I am your bone.
I don't like my solo debut.

However, God is on his throne
        And so far, constantly, he has shown,
through cracks and whispers in the swamp,
        that my loneliness he shares:
living poor, without any pomp,
        heart shot with bullying stares
bleeding red love, like a pump

Guilty

> "He himself bore our sins" in his body on the cross, so that we might die to sins and live for righteousness; "by his wounds you have been healed."
>
> (1 Peter 2:24)

Your Honor, from such a dump
    comes my client!
Apologies for a stark start, Your Honor.
    But from all tautologies,
that's true.
    This man is a goner—
not unlike the big cockroaches
    that offended our juries.
He is guilty, rotten, in decay;
    He has mocked our Law, hurt the small,
wholly lost his reason and way.
    In his fall, he built a tall wall
to keep common sense away.
    He has left us in such dismay!
Should I defend this vermin?
    Could I honestly plead 'not guilty?'
Do your laws predetermine
    we should feel pity for one so filthy?

But, Your Honor, examine
    this proposal: There's famine
around. No grains of justice
    nor is mercy, either, to be found.

I can offer you just this:
    my love for this man, so profound
that I ask you to dismiss him free.
    No, sir! You won't be remiss.
For sure his penalty shall be met
    and his many crimes paid for.
I wouldn't ask you to forget

what's in our justice system's core,
and let the guilty go away. Yet
someone shall pay up his debt.

So be it. Handcuff me, Your Honor!
Willingly I take now his place
for I love him. He's my dear brother
thus I'm offering him my grace.
Aren't you just, Father?

Derelict

Remember your Creator
in the days of your youth,
before the days of trouble come
and the years approach when you will say,
"I find no pleasure in them"
(Ecclesiastes 12:1)

My health was once good. Now it's poor.
    The skin was a mirroring lake,
Nowadays it's the enraged sea
    between joys and mistakes.
"How many?,"
I cannot guarantee I know the number,
    for God's sake!
Now, look at my hands: see how they shake.
    My memories are a jigsaw!
That's my sarcastic existence:
    Eating meat through a damn straw;
Obsessed with the cruel distance
    separating my teeth from my jaw.
(Or from my birth to life's last law.)
    But the knife creeping into my chest
is the dear soul I've lost to fate.
    Without it, how can I rest?
The pain I wish I could sedate
    is excruciating at best.
I'm going on a final quest.
    Stand at the open gateway,
teaching sun, moon, clouds and stars
    on waiting the following day.

Waiting.
Waiting.
Hurting alone,
    thinking: "perhaps it's today!"

They insist my soul's in decay.
    Lost, dead; eaten by local beasts.

Sorry, coloured coat in shreds is not enough.
    My pain refuses that proof.
I've inspected the threads,
    walked over countless streets.
I know that lies come in fleets
    to check and divide;
conquering over sad, hopeless minds.

Not today.
My heart has wings!
    For a light coming through the blinds
reveals my sad soul
praying

“Prepare the way for the Lord,
make straight paths for him.”
(Matthew 3:3)

Layers to God

> He said to them, "It is written,
> 'My house shall be called a house of prayer,'
> but you make it a den of robbers."
> (Matthew 21:13)

"People want to go to church
    But they aren't so just,
Thus they should stay with their bunch
    For saints shouldn't face disgust."

Yet, the people want to try
    But must get past the beggars,
begging for dimes, damned to die
    without help, brothers, carers.

Yet, the beggar wants to go
    But must get past the trader,
Who sells faith—his prices are low
    to help make ends meet easier.

Yet, the trader drops his booth
    But must get past God's saints,
Who've been in church since their youth
    (same prayers, honest complaints.)

Yet, that saint now wants to pray
    But he must get past the priests–
Who enjoy things done their way
    And do fast . . . in between feasts.

Yet, the priest wants to repent
    But must get past the pastor,
who demands his ten per cent,
    despite the masses' disasters.

Yet, the pastor begs salvation
    But must get past the rugged cross,
Which bulldozed through religion
    getting God's grace across

Passiontide

Passiontide

At this, they picked up stones to stone him,
but Jesus hid himself,
slipping away from the temple grounds.
(John 8:59)

After days, I asked Jesus
  "Oh, Lord, please tell me the truth!"
So he did, but I hated it.
  Although a friend, since my youth,
I picked up stones to stone him.
  I hated my friend in my whim
And my hatred no one could soothe.

But then he simply vanished
  Hiding away from my sight
"Lord! Lord! I am such a fool!
  Who am I to try and bite
The Creator of our dropped jaws
  Who gave consciousness claws?"
I sigh. My chest is so tight!

I've been trying to find him,
  Looking for his hideout.
He wasn't in my pet church
  Not in the songs nor the shouts
of the inflamed pop preacher,
  Not with the richest teacher
and his honey-licking mouth.

I went to the library;
  Spent my wage in a bookshop,
But he was not in philosophy
  I saw a man with a mop,
performing Amazing Grace.
  "Where's Christ's hiding place,

my friend?" I asked him nonstop.

He answered: "When I found him
    I was alone in the desert,
Spending time with my own soul."
    I put a lot of effort
Into fighting sun, scorpions,
    Genies, vipers and demons.
Just to find Jesus. Is he hurt?"

> The man answered, "Now that is remarkable!
> You don't know where he comes from,
> yet he opened my eyes."
> (John 9:30)

The desert is now my home.
    I've become a tenant
just about one month or so.
    The moon is exuberant
but it scorches me with remorse.
    The sun, at maximum force,
freezes me with fear.
    I can't stay any longer.
I must leave.
    Because Jesus is not here.
I am my lone companion
    (and one who is not sincere)
Although, when I see a stone,
    o, that chills me to my bones:
I made my friend disappear!

Oh, the shame in my footprints!
    Then a former blind man came
telling me his great story—
    an account destined for fame.
My Jesus handed his sight back.
    The world, previously black,
got a Technicolor frame.

"If you found Jesus, blind man,
    why have you come to this place?"
I asked. Smiling he answered:
"Some come here in their disgrace
    to find a blind way to Christ;
by darkness I was enticed
    to preach of his blinding grace."

I urged him: "You must tell me!
    Why is He invisible?"
He said: "Invisible? No!
    With those who are miserable
he spends his precious time;
    with those viewed as shady slime,
making their lives liveable."

The thief comes only to steal and kill and destroy.
(John 10:10)

"What now? What have you done now?
    Your life was miserable
What's worse than misery?
    On your quest, being unable
to find your 'Dear Saviour'!
    You lost will, heart and grandeur
Your spirit is unstable

Where are you in this your quest?
    On this lonely mountain
With limbs scratched, bruised and broken?
    Come on, don't ignore your brain!
Now, you're in such distraught
    For your efforts add to nought.
No use in starting again

Have you no food for yourself?
    Well, there's plenty of your meat

for careful, howling wolves
        And condors see you: a treat.
Jackals! As a bulldozer,
        closer and closer and closer
Not long now; can't retreat.

But what terrifies you more?
        Do you think the predators just kill you?
You're alive
        when they eat; competitors
Patiently await their turn
        whilst your guilt and your soul burn.
No last prayer, no pastors!"

"I am the good shepherd;
I know my sheep and my sheep know me . . .
(John 10:14)

"Have you given up yet, sheep?
        It's silent and wintry
but my voice is a wildfire.
        I've written History
And you are not dying today.
        I will chase Satan away
Just Wait. I'll set you free."

" . . . Lord, the one you love is sick."
(John 11:3)

So, Schrödinger had a cat.
        He put his cat inside a box;
closed the box, the cat inside—
        A test quite unorthodox.
Linking the box to lethal gas
        with a thin tube made of glass
he put on a button, no clocks.

So, this man comes to the switch
    and presses it—no remorse
but don't start assuming things;
    don't let your voice become hoarse,
emotive for the poor mammal
    because your mind will scramble:
Is the cat alive? Dead perforce?

So, look at me on this cold stone.
    Sheep locked in a butchery
the void of my life, filled with death–
    link to lethal impurity
pulse grasping to a button
    pressed out of a sudden
My life is quantum uncertainty!

Jesus said to her, "I am the resurrection and the life.
The one who believes in me will live, even though they die;
and whoever lives by believing in me will never die.
(John 11:25–26)

"So, "Lazarus," here I am
    That button was pressed by me
And I am glad that you died
    They can see the Almighty
And believe his Son, Jesus—
    truth, not a hypothesis
And live with one certainty:
    The void of death, filled with life;
love, beyond shadows of doubt
    and peace to wage war at sin
My love for you I'll shout:
    I open the box, weeping
And I command you, rejoicing:
    You, live! Lazarus, come out!"

But one of his disciples, Judas Iscariot,

who was later to betray him, objected,
"Why wasn't this perfume sold and the money given to the poor?
(John 12:4–5)

I still remember that day . . .
    I had left my old city,
I had crossed a grey desert
    Met a blind man,
whose mighty vision was a miracle.
    My quest is as biblical
as my spirit was grimy

Was: as in dead, gone, past.
    Rescued from isolation
I now recollect those days
    when I hatched in new creation.
Jesus, surrounded by gurus,
    saw me in rags and crying too.
(Embarrassing situation.)

The masters eyeing me up
    The Master gazing in depth
I had nothing to give him,
    not even my lung's breath
since he had taken it away.
    People, too wise for me, say:
"This vermin! It deserves death!"

Jesus' eyes loved me still.
    So I melted down and broke in
They think they know him!
    His feet had such a thick skin
Blisters that loved me much more
    than the society's wise core
He heard not sobs, but violins

His worker hands on my hair
    had help for a lifetime.

I said I didn't deserve
    it after so many crimes
But He smiled: "I don't care.
    I have love and grace to spare.
Can you believe it? Try me!"

Jesus said to the woman,
"Your faith has saved you; go in peace."
(Luke 7:50)

Gratitude

“. . . whoever has been forgiven little loves little.”
(Luke 7:47)

I truly wanted to say just ‘thank you’,
for money, debt, health, and even the flu.
I tried Portuguese,
English I squeezed,
I couldn’t say anything. But you knew.

The old cliché

> "For God so loved the world, that he gave his only Son,
> that whoever believes in him should not perish
> but have eternal life.
> (John 3:16)

I watched this film
 about ruthless gangsters
and their life's pilasters.
 There was a girl, too slim,
for whom the bloke
 fell in love with—first sight.
Well, an old cliché alright:

Together they sin–
 Wasted lives in the trash bin.

A truth, though, that evokes
 that Love and justice,
in our world,
 walk together as one.

(But Love and justice,
 in our world,
spring from Father and Son)

The Tale of the Trees

Sunday

> The next day the great crowd that had come for the festival heard that Jesus was on his way to Jerusalem. They took palm branches and went out to meet him, shouting, "Hosanna!" "Blessed is he who comes in the name of the Lord!"
>
> "Blessed is the king of Israel!"
>
> (John 12:12–13)

I am a tree. A palm tree.
        I have grown tall, statuesque
my wide leaves were my proud crown
        but mankind is grotesque.
At holy city's doors,
        the feverish crowd just roars–
a scene quite picturesque

I cannot fetch what they say
        But so they come, one by one,
ripping off my stunning leaves.
        What good to me is the sun
if I have no chlorophyll?
        Do you fathom how I feel?
Moreover, when they were done
        I knew I was going to starve
I gave them shade and fruits
        they never gave me water
and then they come taking.
        Brutes!
I wish I could understand
        people; their crazy demands
they are lions but we are newts

Suddenly I see my leaves
        laying flat over the ground
as some kind of red carpet
        with cellulose all around,
I wasn't bothered at all

until I heard this call:
"He's coming! The one renowned
as the dear Root of David!"
They were calling him true vine
grain of wheat, a shoot of hope.
Perhaps he is so divine
that he can be my food source,
my xylem, sap, long lost force.
With him, maybe, all will be fine

So be it, my new Messiah,
I believe in your power.
May my leaves be your cushion.
Be my water, make me flower.
My energy at your feet
although a bit obsolete
is all my glory, Master.

So the Pharisees said to one another,
"See, this is getting us nowhere.
Look how the whole world has gone after him!"
(John 12:19)

MONDAY

> The next day as they were leaving Bethany, Jesus was hungry. Seeing in the distance a fig tree in leaf, he went to find out if it had any fruit. When he reached it, he found nothing but leaves, because it was not the season for figs.
>
> (Mark 11:12–13)

I am a tree. A fig tree.
    However, I have no figs.
It's not the right season
    I don't have enough twigs,
There are no pollinators
    And there are many factors
Yes, many . . . not enough sprigs . . .

Anyway, here's the thing:
    The True Vine was passing by
and he only wanted some figs.
    They didn't have any supply,
To share between beloved friends.
    I couldn't make any amends;
They were hungry. I was dry.

They scrutinized all my branches
    As if they were inspecting
some high quality products
    which I was not offering.
Disappointment is bitter.
    He saw me as a quitter
but I was not admitting.

Why though? Why haven't I
    produced fruits? Even if small?
Not even one! Why, why not?
    Not that I made figs for all
of the brute human species,
    not by will, or entreaties.

It's just . . . I just . . . I stalled

I wanted to employ mankind
        in spreading my seeds across.
I wanted the most perfect tool
        to avert any latent loss
(it was my darn selfish genes)–
        I wanted them in all ravines
around both worker and boss

I never offered any help . . .
        So much so that He cursed me
Cursed me! To wither quickly!
        Cursed me to be a fruit tree
without fruits and without life!
        While my neighbours . . . they thrive!
I couldn't be bothered, me.

I just couldn't be bothered.

In the morning, as they went along,
they saw the fig tree withered from the roots.
(Mark 11:20)

Tuesday

> When it was almost time for the Jewish Passover, Jesus went up to Jerusalem. In the temple courts he found people selling cattle, sheep and doves, and others sitting at tables exchanging money. So he made a whip out of cords, and drove all from the temple courts, both sheep and cattle; he scattered the coins of the money changers and overturned their tables.
>
> (John 2:13–15)

I'm no tree, but a rush.
    Just a simple, trivial rush
I don't even know why.
    I say it without a flush
and I'm okay with that:
    I'm not nice to look at
(but I'm good as a brush)

I spread alongside the road
    homeless at the margin;
I never grew very tall
    I just take it to the chin:
I am here. I do exist.
    Throughout the ages, I persist
whilst everyone is rushing

I get beatings from the wind,
    because I am not that firm;
I bend, I am stepped upon,
    my companion is a worm.
Been rough, but I never cried,
    Forever staying outside
whether it's cold or warm

I almost break with the storm
    when the drops feel more like bombs
Eventually, the sun comes
    but I have to fight the palms

and compete with lazy figs—
    and pray against hungry pigs,
having to live with my qualms.

One day I saw the True Vine
    homeless, at the margin.
His companions seen as worms
    but a violent peace within.
He cursed the lazy fig trees,
    He walked over the palm leaves,
Oddly, He was of my kin

He saw me; he picked me up
    He turned me into a whip;
used me to clean his temple
    "Out with the tare!" Tables flip–
and he whips merchants with me
    I am trivial, but you see,
I would thank him, to my tip.

His disciples remembered that it is written:
"Zeal for your house will consume me."
(John 2:17)

Wednesday

> Then one of the Twelve—the one called Judas Iscariot—went to the chief priests and asked, "What are you willing to give me if I deliver him over to you?" So they counted out for him thirty pieces of silver.
> From then on Judas watched for an opportunity to hand him over.
> (Matthew 26:14–16)

You know I'm a tree. Oak.
        Silent night, unholy night.
Not even wolves are howling.
        All is calm. All is quiet.
The type of gloomy calmness,
        boiling suspense upon us.
Earlier since, since the twilight,
        Nightfall hasn't said "hello."
Tonight all creation is mute,
        Except for some whisperings.
A deal about bloody loot;
        The friend turned to foe;
Sawing of an unknown tree;
        I shiver from leaf to root.
The cursed silver! And for what?

Wait now. Silence! Quiet! Shush!
        The shadows are thick, pitch black.
Birds went from chirping to a hush
        The ghost of the tree murmurs
It wails, faintly, "murderers."
        Wind brings the leaves of rush.
The sunlight from the full moon
        brings inertia, brings stillness
The unbalanced forces tonight
        thank the impulsiveness
of priests, thirsty for a riot.
        Why you, Judas Iscariot?
Capitalist homeless!

Now, my forest, hold vigil.
    They want to burn the True Vine!
Send seeds to the olive trees
    And tell them of the design
Of our master and creator!
    Let them know of the traitor.

Oh Carpenter, friend of mine!
    Remember the day you slept
under shadows of my branches?
    I hope that woman gave you
the myrrh, aloes, nard, and spices
    We've been synthesizing.
Lord, we know where you are going.

But who has felt such distress?

Then Jesus went with his disciples to a place called Gethsemane,
and he said to them, "Sit here while I go over there and pray."
(Matthew 26:36)

Thursday

> Jesus went out as usual to the Mount of Olives, and his disciples followed him. On reaching the place, he said to them, "Pray that you will not fall into temptation." He withdrew about a stone's throw beyond them, knelt down and prayed, "Father, if you are willing, take this cup from me; yet not my will, but yours be done." An angel from heaven appeared to him and strengthened him. And being in anguish, he prayed more earnestly,
> and his sweat was like drops of blood falling to the ground.
> (Luke 22:39–44)

I'm an awed olive tree.
Because underneath my bough,
The True Vine is here, bleeding
His blood is sweat on his brow.
The forest of olives is
jaw-dropped and speechless at this.
He is alone. Alone. How?

He has kneeled before our God
and God, in wrath and sorrow,
is now kneeling upon him.
The pressing is tomorrow
He, a lonely olive,
squeezed hard, with no relief,
and his friends do not follow.
Astonishing. Small olive
being crushed by an asteroid
Can you smell the sweet fragrance?
Weep now! He must be destroyed!
Can you smell his iron sweat?
This very night poses a threat:
A cup he cannot avoid.

The oak told us of tonight–
Fear underestimated.
The Son of God is afraid;

Judas, afraid of being hated;
Satan, afraid of losing;
Mankind, afraid of winning.
Today, Cosmos has deflated.
The Son of God is afraid
His agony: not his cross.
He scoffs at Satan's demons,
He weeps for his friendship lost
And he loves mankind to bits
forgiving the punches, the spits.
Yes, his grace will come across.
His agony is due to
knowing his Father's wrath
He'd been anointed with joy
But unless He takes this path
The pure oil will not come out–
Although it's not his fault,
He'll pay.
He'll do the math.

"Abba, Father," he said, "everything is possible for you.
Take this cup from me. Yet not what I will, but what you will."
(Mark 14:36)

After Jesus said this, he looked toward heaven and prayed: "Father, the hour has come. Glorify your Son, that your Son may glorify you. For you granted him authority over all people that he might give eternal life to all those you have given him. Now this is eternal life: that they know you, the only true God, and Jesus Christ, whom you have sent. I have brought you glory on earth by finishing the work you gave me to do. And now, Father, glorify me in your presence with the glory I had with you before the world began. (John 17:1–5)

Friday

But they shouted,
"Take him away! Take him away! Crucify him!"
"Shall I crucify your king?" Pilate asked.
"We have no king but Caesar," the chief priests answered.
Finally Pilate handed him over to them to be crucified.
(John 19:15–16)

Call me tree. I'm a cross.
    I produce no sap, but blood
I do not make any glucose
    I have neither roots nor bud
I create no fruit, no flower
    I germinated for this hour
I am a dead piece of wood

How many trees had the joy
    of killing a carpenter?
I take no joy in this though;
    Look at his friend. His mother!
The sun barely bears it.
    World's opinion is split—
Such a unique Easter

The oak heard my sad murmur.
    When I was cut off and killed
he confided to the olives
    that I had been frankensteined.
I heard the palm died for him;
    The curse on the fig was grim
Even the rush was honoured!

Someone has just spat on him.
    Why! He has just forgiven!

He is a holy, bleeding vine,

for his fruit has been riven,
His sap is haemoglobin
that will fossilise all sin
He is God's grace given;
He gives God immense glory.
I take no joy in all this . . .
Those two criminals beside?
I would torture in a bliss,
This Son of Man? Innocent.
Humble King. Magnificent!
Why does he desire my kiss?

Explaining why I'm baffled:
I am half-dead. A zombie.
However, he embraced me!
Besides I can guarantee
I came biting all the way
And He knows He dies today . . .

> Later, knowing that everything had now been finished, and so that Scripture would be fulfilled, Jesus said, "I am thirsty." A jar of wine vinegar was there, so they soaked a sponge in it, put the sponge on a stalk of the hyssop plant, and lifted it to Jesus' lips. When he had received the drink, Jesus said, "It is finished."
>
> With that, he bowed his head and gave up his spirit.
>
> (John 19:28–30)

It's over.
You are free.

Good
Friday.
The cross points right up–
Crossed
window.

Saturday

So Joseph bought some linen cloth, took down the body,
wrapped it in the linen, and placed it in a tomb cut out of rock.
Then he rolled a stone against the entrance of the tomb.
Mary Magdalene and Mary the mother of Joseph saw where he was laid.
(Mark 15:46–47)

I am but a seed. What now?
    Do try and leave the service
In a complete, dry silence;
    Then ask about your purpose.
Try any life's direction
    without the Resurrection.
Don't you feel anxious?

. . . they rested on the Sabbath
in obedience to the commandment.
(Luke 23:56)

Lord's Day

Early on the first day of the week, while it was still dark, Mary Magdalene went to the tomb and saw that the stone had been removed from the entrance. (. . .)
Now Mary stood outside the tomb crying.
As she wept, she bent over to look into the tomb . . .
(John 20:1;11)

I am a brand new green sprout,
    and I saw the miracle!
The True Vine, put in the soil
    by a mob, anarchical,
was left alone, mocked, crushed, dead—
    despised as heaven's bread.
Something phenomenal!

His friends put him tenderly
    in the soil, tear-watering,
and went enjoying sadness.
    They didn't see it coming:
that broken and despised dead seed,
    it raised from the dead, indeed–
I witnessed everything

One sad lady came early
    from afar; crossed the city,
passing by the dead palm tree,
    the cursed fig tree (so ugly),
rush leaves made in a whip;
    the wise oak she didn't skip,
The bittersweet olive trees.
    She saw lilies of the field
and asked: "does God really care?"
    She saw seeds embraced by thorns,
dried and dead—so much to bear!
    She saw some boys jumping a fence

running, laughing nonsense,
    throwing away half-eaten pears.
When she saw me, she stopped by.
    Touching my small leaves, she asked:
"What tree are you going to be?
    Truthful one, or rather, masked?
He has told me, my cute sprout,
    when the long-sought fruit comes out
it'll have the same impact."
    Then she heard his charming voice
"Maybe it is the gardener?"
    She said. But I knew better:
The True Vine! He approached her
    and said: "My work here is done.
Now, take care of my Garden, church!
    Shout!
Be the world's myrrh."

The angel said to the women, "Do not be afraid, for I know that you are looking for Jesus, who was crucified. He is not here; he has risen, just as he said. Come and see the place where he lay. Then go quickly and tell his disciples:
'He has risen from the dead and is going ahead of you into Galilee.
There you will see him.' Now I have told you."
(Matthew 28:5–7)

He said to them,
"Go into all the world and preach the gospel to all creation.
Whoever believes and is baptized will be saved,
but whoever does not believe will be condemned. (Mark 16:15–16)

Epilogue

For in this hope we were saved.
But hope that is seen is no hope at all.
Who hopes for what they already have?
(Romans 8:24)

On the other side of the line,
Beyond the Immigration Officer,
There lies my smiling shadow
waiting for me to cross over
Annoyed with my delay.
The officer checks my passport
Asking me so many questions . . .
And the shadow waits.
It's as if it couldn't depart from me!

As the thrill of a new life
Makes my hands shake
I step up.
Is this my new home?
Was I at home?
Am I thrilled or just shivering?
I feel I've done something wrong
and the Officer will eventually discover it,
rubbing it against my face.
But what could that be?
I don't fully understand his language

My shadow. There.

I cross the border
And my shadow shrinks,
And the sun is now in front of me
And my shadow rotates
Ending up behind me–
A direction where I'll

Never look back again
    Who's smiling now?

www.ingramcontent.com/pod-product-compliance
Lightning Source LLC
Chambersburg PA
CBHW071106090426
42737CB00013B/2499

* 9 7 8 1 5 3 2 6 6 4 4 4 1 *